SUCCESS CATALYST

Harnessing Principles for Prosperity and Wealth

Christine M. Dahmen

Copyright

All rights reserved. No part of this publication may be reproduced, distributed, or transmitted in any form or by any means, including photocopying, recording, or other electronic or mechanical methods, without the prior written permission of the publisher, except in the case of brief quotations embodied in critical reviews and certain other noncommercial uses permitted by copyright law.

© [2024] by Christine M. Dahmen

Disclaimer

The information in this book is for general informational purposes only. While we've made every effort to ensure its accuracy and completeness, we make no guarantees about its reliability or suitability for your needs.

We're not liable for any loss or damage you may experience from using the information in this book. Please use your own judgment when applying any strategies or recommendations.

Any product names, trademarks, or service marks mentioned belong to their respective owners and are used for identification purposes only.

By using this book, you agree to these terms.

Christine M. Dahmen

About the Author

Meet Christine M. Dahmen, a force to be reckoned with in the business world enthusiastically for helping other people make progress in their lives. Christine's process is one of assurance, strength, and resolute obligation to greatness.

With a foundation in business, the executives and business, Christine has gone through years leveling up her abilities and excelling at progress. Her own encounters defeating deterrents and accomplishing her objectives genuinely want to share her insight and engage others to arrive at their maximum capacity.

Christine's way to deal with progress is pragmatic, yet well established in standards of self-awareness and advancement. She accepts that everybody has the ability to change their lives and make the future they want. Through her composition, instructing, and talking commitment, Christine rouses and propels people to make a move and seek after their fantasies with certainty and reason.

As an effective financial specialist, Christine figures out the difficulties and open doors that accompany business ventures and initiative. Her bits of knowledge into viable techniques for abundance creation, beating deterrents, and supporting achievement have assisted incalculable people and associations with accomplishing their objectives.

Past her expert accomplishments, Christine is known for her glow, compassion, and real longing to have an effect in the existence of others. She moves toward each cooperation with benevolence and sympathy, establishing a strong climate where individuals feel esteemed and engaged to seek after their objectives.

In her extra energy, Christine appreciates investing time with her family, heading out to new objections, and rewarding her local area through generous undertakings. She puts stock in making every moment count and urges others to do likewise.

With her abundance of information, experience, and energy for helping other people succeed, Christine M. Dahmen is a guiding light for anybody on the way to accomplishing their fantasies. Prepare to be roused, inspired, and enabled to arrive at new levels of accomplishment with Christine's direction close by.

Introduction

The world hushed up in the quietness of day break, the sun scarcely looking into the great beyond. As the morning light leisurely enlightened the way forward, I wound up remaining at the junction of my excursion. This was the second when everything changed, the second when I chose to turn into the impetus of my own prosperity. My way had been cleared with difficulties and mishaps, however not entirely set in stone to produce another course, one that would lead me to an existence of direction, overflow, and satisfaction.

As I set out on this excursion, I understood that I was in good company. Each individual I experienced, each story I heard, talked about dreams and yearnings ready to be understood. Every one of us conveys inside us the flash of potential, the ability to accomplish significance and have an effect on the planet. However, so frequently, we wind up kept down by uncertainty, dread, and vulnerability, uncertain of how to open the way to our own prosperity.

This book, "Success Catalyst", is the summit of my journey to uncover the keys to progress and impart them to other people. It is a guide for the people who try to saddle the standards of riches and success and change their lives. Through a mix of individual stories, genuine models, and useful exhortation, this book fills in as an aide for anybody hoping to light their true capacity and leave on an excursion of self-disclosure and accomplishment.

The excursion to progress isn't clear all of the time. It is loaded up with exciting bends in the road, snapshots of win, and snapshots of misfortune. In any case, exactly these difficulties shape us, form us, and move us forward. "Success Catalyst" is tied in with embracing the excursion, tracking down strength notwithstanding snags, and enduring in any event, when the way appears to be unsure. It is tied in with assuming responsibility for our predeterminations and being the impetuses of our own prosperity.

In the pages that follow, you will track down experiences into the underpinning of progress, investigating the mentality and propensities that set up for accomplishment. We dig into the standards of thriving, looking at how to develop overflow and set out open doors for development. The book likewise takes you through the systems for abundance creation, offering noteworthy stages to fabricate and support monetary security.

Exploring snags is a basic piece of the excursion, and "Success Catalyst" outfits you with the devices to conquer difficulties and transform difficulties into valuable open doors for development. Supporting achievement requires flexibility and versatility, and this book gives direction on the most proficient method to keep up with force and flourish.

Be that as it may, this book is something other than an assortment of standards and systems. It is a source of inspiration, an update that you hold the ability to shape your future. Whether you are toward the start of your excursion or looking to lift your ongoing degree of achievement, "Success Catalyst" offers the motivation and functional direction you really want to make the following stride.

As you leave on this excursion, remember that achievement isn't exclusively characterized by material riches or outer accomplishments. It is tied in with carrying on with an existence of direction, adding to the prosperity of others, and leaving an enduring effect. The genuine proportion of achievement lies in the actual excursion — the illustrations taken in, the connections assembled, and the lives contacted en route.

In this way, as you turn the pages of "Success Catalyst," permit yourself to think ambitiously and ponder the conceivable outcomes that look for you. Allow this book to be your sidekick, your coach, and your aide as you explore the way to progress. Embrace the excursion, and recall that you are the impetus of your own fate. The ability to accomplish significance exists in you — this is the ideal opportunity to release it.

Acknowledgement

As I ponder the excursion of composing Success Catalyst, I'm loaded up with massive appreciation for the many individuals who played an urgent influence in its creation. This book is the finish of long stretches of learning, development, and motivation, and it could never have been conceivable without the help and direction of others.

Above all else, I'm profoundly thankful to the significant creators whose work in the field of business, self-improvement, and achievement has significantly affected my life. To names, for example, Napoleon Slope, Stephen R. Flock, and Dale Carnegie, your immortal bits of knowledge have been a signal of light, directing me through the intricacies of making progress. Your insight has been instrumental in molding how I might interpret the rules that drive individual and expert development.

I should likewise communicate my sincere appreciation to my family, whose steady help has been my establishment all through this excursion. To my folks, thank you for imparting in me the upsides of difficult work, versatility, and uprightness. Your faith in my capacities has powered my assurance to seek after my fantasies.

To my accomplice, your support, persistence, and love have been a steady wellspring of solidarity. You have been close by through each late evening of composing and each snapshot of uncertainty. Your help has had a significant effect, and I'm genuinely thankful.

To my companions and coaches, thank you for your important guidance, productive criticism, and motivation. Your bits of knowledge have enhanced my point of view and moved me to ponder the ideas investigated in this book.

At long last, I might want to thank my pursuers. It is my true expectation that Achievement Impetus fills in as a wellspring of motivation and strengthening on your own excursion to progress. Your help and energy propel me to keep sharing information and bits of knowledge that can decidedly affect your lives.

To all who have added to the making of this book, whether straightforwardly or by implication, thank you sincerely. Your impact has been a necessary piece of my excursion, and I'm regarded to impart the products of that excursion to you.

With appreciation,

[Christine M. Dahmen]

CONTENTS

Introduction

CONTENTS

Part I	**1**
Groundwork of Progress	**1**
Part II	**10**
Standards of Thriving	**11**
Part III	**23**
Systems for Abundance Creation	**23**
Part IV	**33**
Exploring Snags	**33**
Part V	**43**
Supporting Achievement	**43**
CONCLUSION	**57**

Part I

Groundwork of Progress

Clarity of Course

The North Star of Achievement

In the colossal extent of the universe, each boat needs a guiding star to investigate through the obscurity. Additionally, in the journey of life, clearness of course fills in as our coordinating star, illuminating the way forward and guiding us towards our goal. In this part, we will examine the meaning of clearness of bearing in laying out the basis for progress.

Tracking down Your Why

At the center of clearness of course lies the chief inquiry: why are we and we doing likewise? Seeing as our why is essential for changing our exercises to our most significant characteristics and wants. Through mindfulness and reflection, we can uncover the basic aims that drive us and gain clarity on our inspiration all through regular daily existence.

Characterizing Clear Targets

At the point when we have clarity of course, the ensuing stage is to make an understanding of our vision into huge targets. Setting clear, unequivocal, and quantifiable goals licenses us to gain an aide for headway and monitor our improvement in transit. We will examine strategies for characterizing Smart targets that are Express, Quantifiable, Reachable, Significant, and Time-bound.

Agreeing with Reason

Accomplishment isn't just about achieving targets; it's connected to living in the course of action with our inspiration reliably. Changing our exercises, decisions, and necessities with our inspiration ensures that we stay on target and convinced even in spite of troubles. We will discuss sensible techniques for agreeing with reason and staying reliable with our vision.

Advancement Viewpoint

In the trip towards progress, our viewpoint expects a vital part in shaping our outcomes. An improvement viewpoint, portrayed by a confidence in the power of learning and flexibility, is key for vanquishing obstacles, embracing challenges, and opening our most extreme limit. In this part, we will examine the principles of advancement mindset and their impact on progress.

Embracing Challenges

As opposed to fearing dissatisfaction, individuals with an improvement mindset believe troubles to be open entryways for advancement and learning. They embrace setbacks as wandering stones to advance and push toward obstacles with strength and confirmation. We will inspect methods for embracing hardships, reexamining incidents, and fostering a mindset of adaptability.

Creating Adaptability

Adaptability is the ability to get back from trouble more grounded, not completely firmly established than beforehand. An indispensable nature of viable individuals progresses forward regardless of incidents and disasters. We will examine strategies for building adaptability, such as encouraging a moving viewpoint, practicing, dealing with oneself, and searching for help from others.

Predictable Learning and Improvement

Accomplishment is certainly not a target yet a trip of constant learning and improvement. Individuals with an improvement standpoint are centered around enduring learning and believe powerlessness to be input for advancement. We will inspect the meaning of searching for analysis, investigating various roads in regards to pivotal contemplations, and embracing a mindset of predictable improvement.

In the Preparation of Achievement, we dig significantly into the bedrock whereupon all achievements are developed. It's here that we uncover the significant guidelines that help each compelling endeavor. As we research this area, we're setting out on a journey of self-divulgence and change, coordinated by the eternal knowledge that has formed the destinies of boundless visionaries since the dawn of time.

Clearness of Bearing is the groundwork of this foundation, filling in as the coordinating light that edifies our far ahead. With clarity comes focus, heading, and an internal compass that infuses every movement with significance and assumption. It's connected to understanding what we want to achieve, but why it has an effect on us on a significant, trademark level. Exactly when we change our targets to our core values and convictions, we tap into a wellspring of motivation and adaptability that moves us towards our objectives.

Be that as it may, clearness alone isn't adequate. We ought to moreover foster an Improvement Viewpoint — a steadfast trust in our capacity to learn, change, and fill despite challenges. This mindset empowers us to consider setbacks to be any entryways for improvement, hardships as wandering stones to headway, and frustration as a temporary redirection making a course for strength. It's connected to embracing the journey of learning and improvement with extraordinary friendship, seeing that every obstruction is a consolation to turn out to be more grounded, more brilliant, and more grounded.

In this trip of self-disclosure, we're not just uninvolved observers — we're dynamic individuals in the development of our own fates. Through care, reflection, and care, we uncover the further experiences that portray what our character is and a major inspiration for us. We go facing our sensations of fear, questions, and vulnerabilities head-on, recalling that they are not as tangles to be made due, yet rather as any entryways for advancement and change.

As we investigate the scene of the Supporting of Progress, we're coordinated by an internal compass and a promise to significance. We're fueled by an enthusiastic yearning to affect the planet and withdraw a getting through legacy that transcends our solitary achievements. Besides, with each step we take, we're reminded that accomplishment isn't simply a goal — it's an outing of steady turn of events, divulgence, and discipline.

So let us embrace the trial of building our support of progress bit by bit, rule by rule. Permit us to dare to dream enormous, act seriously, and seek after our inclinations with unwavering affirmation. For in the cauldron of difficulty, we track down the authentic extent of our fortitude. Moreover, pursuing our dreams, we open the unfathomable chance that exists in all of us.

Part II

Standards of Thriving

1. Rule of Action

- Action as an impulse for changing dreams into this present reality.
- The meaning of deliberate, unequivocal steps towards goals.
- Making the most of the open door and embracing force.

2. Rule of Constancy

- Consistent quality in spite of impediments, hardships, and troubles.
- Supporting commitment to the journey for goals.
- Declining to be put by fleeting accidents down.

3. Rule of Flood

- Seeing the unending flood that incorporates us.
- Fostering a demeanor of appreciation and party.
- Granting flood to others and embracing "all that anybody could require."

4. Rule of Course of action

- Fitting examinations, convictions, and exercises with needs and objectives.
- Living in uprightness with individual characteristics and reason.
- Earnestly committing to critical responsibilities agreed with our soul's calling.

Examination of Guidelines of Progress

In diving into the Guidelines of Progress, we uncover an overflow of encounters, techniques, and practices that empower us to make lives of flood and fulfillment. From fostering a flood mindset to using the example of good following great, each standard offers an aide for opening our fullest potential and grasping our most significant desires. At last, veritable overflow is found not in material possessions, yet rather in the luxury of our experiences, the significance of our associations, and the legacy we leave.

In researching the "Success Catalyst," we set out on a huge trip into the genuine substance of wealth and flood. A journey transcends basic material assets and plunges into the more significant progressions of human fulfillment and thriving. As we investigate this region, we experience a weaving of decisions that structure the design blocks of a day to day presence stacked up with flourishing, reason, and importance.

At the center of the Success Catalyst lies the Rule of Movement — an essential truth that features the meaning of taking intentional, unequivocal steps towards our goals. Movement is the stimulus that changes dreams into this present reality, objectives into achievements, and potential into execution. It's connected to making the most of the open door, harnessing our internal resources, and embracing the power of energy to move us towards our optimal outcomes.

Nonetheless, action alone isn't adequate. We ought to similarly embrace the Rule of Eagerness — the enduring commitment to drive forward even with checks, disasters, and troubles. Creativity is the fuel that upholds us through the difficulties of life, engaging us to confront the difficulties and emerge more grounded, more intelligent, and more grounded on the contrary side. It's connected to declining to be forestalled by brief accidents and staying reliable with our vision, regardless, when the way forward seems, by all accounts, to be problematic.

Key to the Principles of Progress is the Rule of Flood — a huge affirmation of the unending flood that envelops us and the limitless entryways that exist in our grasp. Flood isn't just a mindset; it's a way to deal with being — a significant acknowledgment that there is all that anybody could require to go around and that we are justifying all of the blessings that life offers that would be useful. It's connected to fostering a mindset of appreciation, commending the blessings in our lives, and conferring our flood to others.

In embracing the Principles of Flourishing, we similarly experience the Rule of Plan — the specialty of arranging our examinations, convictions, and exercises with our most significant longings and desires. Plan is connected to living in decency with our characteristics, in regards to our genuine selves, and staying reliable with our inspiration, regardless, when defied with external strains and suppositions. It's connected to finding our striking spot in the world and sincerely committing to a huge responsibility that reverberates with our soul.

As we dive further into the Norms of Progress, we uncover a treasure trove of pieces of information, frameworks, and practices that draw in us to make a presence of flood and fulfillment. From fostering a spilling over standpoint to embracing the power of appreciation, from using the example of good following great to outfitting the powers of sign, each rule offers an aide for opening our fullest potential and grasping our most significant desires.

Ultimately, the Norms of Accomplishment exhort us that certified overflow isn't assessed by the size of our records or the effects we accumulate, but by the sumptuousness of our experiences, the significance of our associations, and the legacy we leave. It's connected to living with reason, energy, and significance, and having a useful result in the world that connects quite far past our own lifetime.

So let us embrace the Principles of Flourishing with open hearts and responsive standpoints, understanding that certified flood isn't something we secure — it's something we epitomize. Moreover, as we adjust to the principles of progress, we open the approaches to a day to day presence spilling over with joy, fulfillment, and interminable entryways for improvement and expansion.

In our journey through the Norms of Flourishing, we uncover huge experiences that illuminate the way to a presence of flood and fulfillment. Each rule fills in as a coordinating reference point, uncovering knowledge into the major parts that add to our prosperity and thriving.

At the focal point of flourishing lies the Standard of Movement — a power that drives us forward while heading to our dreams. Action isn't just a means to an end; it is the real encapsulation of progress and improvement. By taking intentional steps towards our targets, we outfit the power of energy and start off a chain reaction of positive change. Through action, we change our objectives into obvious results and lay out the basis for a presence of flood.

Indeed, even with difficulty and weakness, the Standard of Dauntlessness transforms into our fearless accomplice. Steadiness is the fuel that upholds us through the inescapable troubles of life, enabling us to get through pursuing our dreams. It is the resolute commitment to our vision, regardless, when the road ahead gives off an impression of being long and relentless. Through adaptability and affirmation, we rout obstacles and emerge more grounded, savvier, and more grounded than beforehand.

Integral to the Standards of Thriving is the Rule of Overflow — a comprehension that there is all that anyone could need to go around and that we are meriting every one of the endowments that life brings to the table. Overflow is definitely not a restricted asset to be stored; a perspective commends the wealth of our encounters and the liberality of the universe. By developing a demeanor of appreciation and liberality, we draw in flourishing into our lives and make a gradually expanding influence of overflow that contacts every one of the people around us.

As we continue looking for success, the Guideline of Arrangement becomes vital. Arrangement is tied in with living as one with our actual selves and regarding our most profound longings and desires. It is the most common way of adjusting our considerations, convictions, and activities with our guiding principle and reason, in this manner making a feeling of cognizance and honesty in our lives. Through arrangement, we tap into the boundless insight of our inward direction and release our maximum capacity to make the existence of our fantasies.

As we coordinate these standards into our lives, we set out on an excursion of change and self-disclosure. We figure out how to confide in the inborn overflow of the universe and to embrace the force of our own organization to shape our predeterminations. Through cognizant activity, flexibility despite misfortune, and arrangement with our most profound qualities, we open the ways to an existence of flourishing, satisfaction, and euphoria.

Part III

Systems for Abundance Creation

Building a Monetary Fort

At the core of the quest for success lies the journey for monetary security and overflow. In investigating "Systems for Abundance Creation," we set out on an excursion to open the mysteries of building enduring success and independence from the rat race. From judicious cash the board to insightful speculation procedures, every methodology fills in as a venturing stone towards the acknowledgment of our monetary objectives and yearnings.

Dominating Monetary Education

Monetary education is the foundation of abundance creation — the establishment whereupon any remaining procedures are fabricated. It incorporates the information and abilities important to actually oversee cash, spending plans admirably, and settle on informed monetary choices. By dominating the standards of planning, saving, and money management, we lay the basis for long haul monetary achievement and security.

Contributing Admirably: The Force of Accumulated dividends

One of the most remarkable techniques for abundance creation is financial planning carefully. Whether in stocks, bonds, land, or other resource classes, contributing permits us to develop our abundance dramatically over the long run through the force of accumulating funds. By outfitting the standards of enhancement, risk the board, and long haul financial planning, we can construct a portfolio that creates automated revenue and jelly our abundance for people in the future.

Creating Supportable Financial momentum: The Significance of Recurring, automated revenue

Automated revenue is the way to independence from the rat race — the means by which we can get away from the pattern of exchanging time for cash and accomplish genuine riches and overflow. By making various surges of automated revenue, like rental pay, profits, eminences, and business benefits, we can create abundance that proceeds to develop and compound, in any event, when we're not effectively working.

Utilizing Organizations and Connections

Chasing after abundance creation, our organizations and connections are significant resources. By developing solid associations with tutors, companions, and industry pioneers, we get close enough to significant open doors, assets, and experiences that can speed up our way to progress. Organizing isn't just about building a rundown of contacts — it's tied in with sustaining certifiable connections based on trust, correspondence, and common help.

Embracing Development and Business venture

Advancement and business are strong impetus for abundance creation, offering boundless open doors for development and extension. By distinguishing neglected needs, taking care of issues, and making an incentive for other people, business visionaries can create effective organizations that produce financial wellbeing and make positive change on the planet.

Embracing an enterprising attitude permits us to consider new ideas, proceed with reasonable courses of action, and take advantage of chances for development and development.

In the domain of abundance creation, there exists a powerful exchange of techniques, each contributing its remarkable pith to the quest for monetary success. Past the traditional ideal models of planning and saving falsehoods an immense scene of chances ready to be investigated and bridled. It is inside this scene that we uncover the key to creating enduring financial stability and monetary security.

At the core of abundance creation lies the guideline of monetary proficiency — a key comprehension of how cash functions and how to make it work for us. It is through monetary education that we gain the information and abilities important to explore the complicated universe of individual budgets, from overseeing obligation and credit to understanding speculation choices and retirement arranging. Equipped with this information, we engage ourselves to pursue informed choices that lay the preparation for long haul monetary achievement.

In any case, monetary proficiency alone isn't sufficient. To really tackle the influence of abundance creation, we should likewise embrace the standards of vital money management. Vital putting goes past essentially placing cash into stocks or land — it includes cautious examination, exploration, and intending to recognize valuable open doors that offer the best potential for development and profit from speculation. Whether it's investigating developing business sectors, putting resources into imaginative innovations, or expanding our portfolio to relieve risk, vital money management permits us to amplify our growing a strong financial foundation potential and accomplish our monetary objectives.

Notwithstanding essential financial planning, one more key technique for abundance creation is the development of automated sources of income. Recurring, automated revenue — cash procured with insignificant exertion or continuous work — gives a steady groundwork to monetary security and opportunity. Whether it's through investment properties, sovereignties from imaginative works, or profits from ventures, automated revenue permits us to produce abundance that proceeds to develop and intensify over the long haul, giving us the opportunity to seek after our interests and carry on with life according to our own preferences.

Be that as it may, maybe the most impressive procedure for abundance creation is the development of an enterprising attitude. Business offers boundless open doors for development and advancement, permitting us to make esteem, tackle issues, and produce abundance on a scale that surpasses our most out of this world fantasies. Whether it's starting a startup, constructing a business realm, or spearheading new innovations, business enables us to shape our own predetermination and make the existence of overflow and thriving that we want.

Eventually, abundance creation isn't just about gathering cash — it's tied in with making a heritage, leaving an enduring effect, and carrying on with an existence of direction and satisfaction. By embracing the standards of monetary proficiency, key money management, recurring, automated revenue age, and business, we can graph a course towards monetary thriving and overflow, opening the ways to a future loaded up with limitless conceivable outcomes and endless potential.

Part IV

Exploring Snags

Exploring impediments is an unavoidable piece of the excursion towards progress and success. Despite difficulties, mishaps, and difficulty, our capacity to explore these obstructions with flexibility, boldness, and assurance frequently decides our definitive result. In this investigation of "Exploring Snags," we dig into the procedures, outlooks, and practices that enable us to conquer affliction and arise more grounded, savvier, and stronger on the opposite side.

Figuring out the Idea of Impediments

Deterrents come in many structures — whether they're outside difficulties, for example, monetary mishaps, medical problems, or professional misfortunes, or inward impediments like self-uncertainty, dread, or restricting convictions. No matter what their tendency, obstructions have the ability to crash our advancement, hose our spirits, and shake our certainty. However, they likewise present us with a chance for development, learning, and self-revelation.

Developing Flexibility

At the core of exploring impediments lies the standard of strength — the capacity to quickly return from misfortune more grounded, not entirely set in stone than previously. Versatility isn't tied in with abstaining from difficulties or denying their effect; it's turning around them head-on, recognizing our feelings, and tracking down the solidarity to persist notwithstanding trouble. By developing flexibility, we foster the inward guts to endure life's hardships and arise victorious on the opposite side.

Transforming Misfortunes into Potential open doors

Notwithstanding misfortune, mishaps can feel like difficult detours holding up traffic of our fantasies. However, mishaps additionally present us with a chance for development and change. By reexamining difficulties as any open doors for learning and personal growth, we can extricate important illustrations from our encounters and use them to move us forward on our excursion. Each difficulty is a venturing stone to progress, an opportunity to recalibrate our course and produce another way towards our objectives.

Adjusting to Change

In a universe of consistent motion and vulnerability, the capacity to adjust to change is fundamental for exploring snags and flourishing notwithstanding difficulty. Versatility is tied in with embracing the obscure, remaining adaptable notwithstanding vulnerability, and tracking down effective fixes to unexpected difficulties. By embracing change as a characteristic piece of life's excursion, we can explore obstructions with elegance and strength, realizing that each diversion carries us nearer to our objectives.

Returning quickly More grounded

Eventually, the genuine proportion of our capacity to explore hindrances lies not in that frame of mind to keep away from them by and large, but rather in our ability to return quickly, more grounded and stronger than previously. Each impediment we experience is a potential chance to test our cutoff points, push past our usual range of familiarity, and find the profundities of our solidarity and strength. By embracing obstructions as any open doors for development and change, we can rise out of difficulty more grounded, smarter, and more able than any other time in recent memory.

In the maze of life, impediments frequently arise as surprising exciting bends in the road that test our determination and challenge our soul. They manifest in horde structures, from unexpected mishaps to overwhelming road obstructions, each introducing a remarkable chance for development and self-disclosure. In our investigation of "Exploring Snags," we leave on an excursion of flexibility, boldness, and change — an excursion that engages us to conquer difficulty and arise more grounded, savvier, and stronger than previously.

As we explore the landscape of obstructions, we stand up to the basic truth that affliction is an unavoidable piece of the human experience. Whether it's an individual mishap, an expert test, or a worldwide emergency, deterrents have the ability to disturb our arrangements, break our fantasies, and shake our feeling of safety. However, it is even with misfortune that our actual strength and character are uncovered. It is through affliction that we are offered the chance to transcend our conditions, go up against our feelings of dread, and tap into the repositories of boldness and versatility that exist in us.

One of the most remarkable systems for exploring deterrents is the act of reevaluating — moving our viewpoint to see difficulties not as unrealistic obstructions, but rather as any open doors for development and learning. By rethinking snags as venturing stones to progress, we can change misfortune into fuel for our excursion, utilizing it to drive us forward as opposed to keep us down. This change in outlook engages us to move toward snags with positive thinking and flexibility, realizing that each mishap is an opportunity to become more grounded, savvier, and more competent than previously.

One more fundamental part of exploring deterrents is the act of versatility — the capacity to quickly return from difficulty with effortlessness and assurance. Flexibility isn't tied in with abstaining from difficulties or denying their effect; it's turning around them head-on, recognizing our feelings, and tracking down the internal solidarity to drive forward notwithstanding trouble. By developing flexibility, we foster strength to face life's hardships and arise victorious on the opposite side, more grounded and stronger than previously.

Notwithstanding versatility, flexibility is likewise urgent for exploring impediments actually. In a universe of steady change and vulnerability, the capacity to adjust to new conditions and turn when vital is fundamental for conquering impediments and accomplishing our objectives. By embracing change as a characteristic piece of life's excursion, we can explore snags, no sweat and adaptability, realizing that each challenge gives us a chance for development and self-revelation.

At last, the excursion of exploring impediments isn't just about defeating misfortune — it's tied in with embracing the course of development and change that accompanies it. It's tied in with figuring out how to see snags not as detours, but rather as venturing stones on the way to our fantasies. What's more, it's tied in with tackling the force of flexibility, versatility, and rethinking to explore life's difficulties with elegance, fortitude, and strength. Despite misfortune, let us recall that inside each obstruction lies the seed of chance — the valuable chance to turn into our best selves and to carry on with an existence of direction, energy, and satisfaction.

Part V

Supporting Achievement

Self-Care and Well-Being

"Supporting Achievement" is the apex of any excursion towards accomplishment. It addresses the capacity to keep up with and expand upon the achievements and energy acquired through difficult work, commitment, and constancy. In this investigation, we dive into the procedures, mentalities, and practices that engage people and associations to support accomplishment over the long haul, guaranteeing progress with development, satisfaction, and effect.

Embracing Nonstop Improvement

One of the keys to supporting achievement is a pledge to ceaseless improvement. Achievement isn't an objective however an excursion, and there is dependably space for development and improvement. By embracing an outlook of constant improvement, you can remain on top of things, adjust to evolving conditions, and persistently hoist your presentation.

Developing a Development Mentality

Integral to supporting achievement is the development of a development mentality — a conviction that your capacities and knowledge can be created through devotion and difficult work. Individuals with a development mentality consider difficulties to be valuable open doors for development and view disappointment as a transitory mishap, not a long-lasting condition. By developing a development outlook, you can beat snags, gain from your encounters, and proceed to develop and work on over the long haul.

Building Strength and Versatility

Even with affliction and difficulties, flexibility and versatility are fundamental characteristics for supporting achievement. Strength is the capacity to return from difficulties, disappointments, and disillusionments, while versatility is the ability to conform to new conditions and flourish in an evolving climate. By building strength and flexibility, you can endure the hardships of existence with effortlessness and arise more grounded and stronger on the opposite side.

Keeping up with Concentration and Discipline

Keeping up with concentration and discipline is vital for supporting accomplishment over the long haul. It's not difficult to become occupied by new open doors or diverted surprising difficulties, however remaining consistent with your objectives and needs is fundamental for keeping focused. By defining clear objectives, making a game plan, and keeping up with discipline in your everyday propensities and schedules, you can guarantee that you keep on gaining ground towards your goals.

Supporting Connections and Organizations

Achievement is definitely not a singular excursion — a cooperative exertion depends on the help and help of others. Sustaining connections and organizations is fundamental for supporting achievement, as they offer significant help, direction, and valuable open doors for development. By putting investment into building and keeping up with positive associations with partners, guides, and friends, you can make areas of strength for a framework that will assist you with exploring difficulties and jump all over new chances.

Adjusting Work and Life

Finding a harmony between your expert and individual life is fundamental for supporting achievement and keeping up with generally prosperity. It's not difficult to become involved with the quest for progress and disregard different parts of your life, however obvious satisfaction comes from accomplishing an amicable harmony between work, family, wellbeing, and recreation. By focusing on taking care of oneself, defining limits, and setting aside a few minutes for the things that make the biggest difference, you can support your prosperity while partaking in a satisfying and significant life.

Focusing on Taking care of oneself and Prosperity

In the midst of the buzzing about day to day existence, focusing on taking care of oneself and prosperity is vital. Dealing with your physical, mental, and close to home wellbeing is fundamental for supporting outcomes over the long haul. Set aside a few minutes for exercises that support your spirit, whether it's activity, contemplation, side interests, or investing energy with friends and family. Make sure to pay attention to your body and brain, and go ahead and back or expert assistance when required. At the point when you focus on taking care of oneself, you'll have the energy and flexibility to handle difficulties and keep flourishing in all aspects of your life.

Legacy and Impact

Figuring out Progress as an Excursion, Not an Objective

Achievement isn't an endpoint yet rather a ceaseless excursion of development and improvement. It includes continuous learning, variation, and refinement. Embracing this viewpoint permits people and associations to stay open to new open doors, difficulties, and opportunities for development.

Developing a Culture of Greatness

A culture of greatness cultivates a climate where exclusive expectations, respectability, and persistent improvement are esteemed and supported. It includes imparting a mentality of greatness in each part of work, from individual undertakings to hierarchical works on, driving execution and guaranteeing that quality remaining parts a first concern.

Embracing Development and Flexibility

Development and versatility are fundamental for remaining pertinent and serious in a quickly impacting world. By cultivating a culture that empowers inventiveness, trial and error, and hazard taking, people and associations can recognize new open doors, expect market moves, and answer proactively to change, guaranteeing progress with progress and development.

Sustaining Flexibility and Dexterity

Flexibility and Dexterity are basic characteristics for exploring difficulties and misfortunes really.

Versatility includes returning from misfortune, gaining from disappointments, and keeping an uplifting perspective despite hardships. Deftness, then again, is the capacity to turn rapidly and actually because of evolving conditions, empowering people and associations to adjust their techniques and plans on a case by case basis to keep on track.

Cultivating Cooperation and Strengthening

Cooperation and strengthening are key drivers of progress, as they saddle the aggregate abilities, thoughts, and energies of people towards shared objectives. By making a culture of joint effort where people feel esteemed, upheld, and engaged to contribute their extraordinary viewpoints and gifts, associations can open innovativeness, development, and superior execution, driving achievement and accomplishing shared targets.

Embracing Consistent Improvement

One of the keys to supporting achievement is a guarantee to nonstop improvement. Achievement isn't an objective yet an excursion, and there is dependably space for development and improvement. By embracing a mentality of persistent improvement, you can remain on top of things, adjust to evolving conditions, and consistently raise your exhibition.

Developing a Development Outlook

Vital to supporting achievement is the development of a development outlook — a conviction that your capacities and insight can be created through commitment and difficult work. Individuals with a development outlook consider difficulties to be potential open doors for development and view disappointment as a transitory difficulty, not a long-lasting condition. By developing a development mentality, you can defeat hindrances, gain from your encounters, and proceed to advance and work on over the long run.

Building Flexibility and Versatility

Despite affliction and difficulties, versatility and flexibility are fundamental characteristics for supporting achievement. Versatility is the capacity to return from difficulties, disappointments, and disillusionments, while flexibility is the ability to conform to new conditions and flourish in an evolving climate.

By building flexibility and versatility, you can face the hardships of existence with beauty and arise more grounded and stronger on the opposite side.

Keeping up with Concentration and Discipline

Keeping up with concentration and discipline is significant for supporting accomplishment over the long haul. It's not difficult to become diverted by new open doors or derailed surprising difficulties, yet remaining consistent with your objectives and needs is fundamental for keeping focused. By defining clear objectives, making a strategy, and keeping up with discipline in your everyday propensities and schedules, you can guarantee that you keep on gaining ground towards your goals.

Sustaining Connections and Organizations

Achievement is certainly not a single excursion — a cooperative exertion depends on the help and help of others. Supporting connections and organizations is fundamental for supporting achievement, as they offer important help, direction, and open doors for development. By putting investment into building and keeping up with positive associations with partners, guides, and companions, you can make major areas of strength for a framework that will assist you with exploring difficulties and quickly jump all over new chances.

CONCLUSION

Releasing Your Internal Catalyst for Success

As we come to the completion of our trip through the pages of "Success Catalyst," we stand at the constraint of credibility, empowered by the data, pieces of information, and adroitness that have edified our direction. In these parts, we have researched the fundamental norms of achievement, dove into the frameworks for overflow creation, and investigated the obstacles that undeniably arise gaining ground toward flourishing.

All through our examination, one truth has remained reliable: accomplishment is definitely not a goal to be reached, but an outing to be embraced — a journey of advancement, change, and self-disclosure. It isn't described by outside respects or material assets, yet by the luxury of our experiences, the significance of our associations, and the impact we make in the presence of others.

At the center of "Success Catalyst" lies the affirmation that all of us have inside us the capacity to be catalysts for our own flourishing. We are not basic spectators in the spreading out demonstration of our lives, yet unique individuals, co-creators of our fates. By harnessing the guidelines of clearness, reason, and movement, we can chart a course towards our goals with sureness and conviction, understanding that we can shape our own reality.

Nevertheless, accomplishment isn't achieved in separation — it is created through collaboration, neighborhood, affiliation. As we adventure forward, let us review the meaning of lifting others as we move, of sharing our knowledge, resources, and experiences to motivate everybody around us. For it is in giving that we truly get, and in empowering others that we draw in ourselves.

As we bid farewell to these pages, let us convey forward the outlines taken in, the pieces of information obtained, and the inspiration lit inside us. Permit us to embrace the journey of accomplishment with open hearts and responsive standpoints, understanding that each challenge we face, every trouble we experience, is an opportunity for improvement, learning, and change.

May "Success Catalyst" go about as a kind of perspective mark of light on your trip towards importance, guiding you through the dimness, energizing you to show up at new levels, and empowering you to deliver the most extreme limit that exists in you. For you are the stimulus for your own success — the architect of your fate, the master of your predetermination. Additionally, with mental determination, confirmation, and adaptability, there is no limitation to what you can achieve.

www.ingramcontent.com/pod-product-compliance
Lightning Source LLC
Chambersburg PA
CBHW050236230526
45470CB00005B/1975